THE UNMOORING

Also by Adebe DeRango-Adem

Ex Nihilo (Frontenac House, 2010)
(co-editor) *Other Tongues: Mixed-Race Women Speak Out*
(Inanna Publications, 2010)
Terra Incognita (Inanna Publications, 2015)

THE UNMOORING

ADEBE DERANGO-ADEM

Mansfield Press

Printed in Canada

Library and Archives Canada Cataloguing in Publication

DeRango-Adem, Adebe, 1986-, author
The unmooring / Adebe DeRango-Adem.

Poems.
ISBN 978-1-77126-160-9 (softcover)

I. Title.

PS8607.E7145U56 2017 C811'.6 C2017-906384-7

Typesetting & Cover Design: Denis De Klerck
Cover Image: Pixabay

The publication of *The Unmooring* has been generously supported by the Canada Council for the Arts and the Ontario Arts Council.

ONTARIO ARTS COUNCIL
CONSEIL DES ARTS DE L'ONTARIO
an Ontario government agency
un organisme du gouvernement de l'Ontario

Canada Council for the Arts Conseil des arts du Canada

Mansfield Press Inc.
25 Mansfield Avenue, Toronto, Ontario, Canada M6J 2A9
Publisher: Denis De Klerck
www.mansfieldpress.net

To my family

TABLE OF CONTENTS

NATIONS FLOAT

O SEA OF TROUBLES WE DID NOT TAKE ARMS AGAINST 11
TREADING WATER 12
ODES TO ALTERITY: OR LIFE BETWEEN THE WAVES 13
LETTER TO THE BELOVED 17
LET US COMPARE COSMOLOGIES 18
TO JOSEPHINE, MY DEAREST SEA NYMPH 19
MISSISSIPPI GOTHIC 20
THE MOOR'S LAMENT 21
DÉJÀ VOODOO 22
BLACK HUMOUR(S) 23
WAXING GOLD 24
GRAVITY & GRACE 25

TIME IS A WHITE LIE, TRAVEL A VEIL

O SAY CAN YOU SEA 31
GHOSTS OF POMPEII 32
THE CAPTURED SIREN 34
THE RECKONING 35
LIBERTY SHELL / I HEAR THE OCEAN 37
TEETOTALING STUDY 42
UNDERWATER IMPALE: OR, A CONJURING 47
IN THE WAKE 50
THE UNMOORING: A PRELUDE 52

ACKNOWLEDGEMENTS 59

NATIONS FLOAT

O SEA OF TROUBLES WE DID NOT TAKE ARMS AGAINST

for many moons we were complete
how beautiful we drifted
were the times we pretended not to bear
of a hollow earth
not a river but a collection of
a clever mix of love
a longing
into a longing to disappear somehow
softening, from the dusts of the
skylines—do you remember
in mangled ways
being in our element
life
wading waiting
the answer is that
to haunt or to be haunted
is the question

like a single river
        & how delirious
        the thirst
as such perhaps we were
rapids & yet those pangs
& fear of the real
        soon to transform
into the familiar
        world
            how we slept
looking out to the Atlantic
but no I will not spend my

        wading
I have arrived with scars

TREADING WATER

every treasure chest breathes heavy
every black pearl understands
the uncomfortable whole
just as every siren knows
to turn her sadness into song
develop a taste for archeology
instinctively come up for air
to surface to herself
watch the lobe of the moon disrobe
consider drowning the dusk's
last brood of sailors
with the stark anthropology of her fins
she finds it amusing
that her tears never get seen
& so taught herself to cope
by hoping deep & long
choosing what's buoyant
learning *so long*

ODES TO ALTERITY: OR LIFE BETWEEN THE WAVES

I.

even this siren forgets
to swim sometimes or see
life's watershed

moments as benediction in disguise
endure
the uncanny cerulean
of things

reckon with the undertow
of the self's grotto opening

mud-colored women floating
over night waters, loving deeply
like reckless wreckage singing
songs of nothing to lose

II.

having tasted destiny too early I
decided to train the otters
of my mind to work toward
more than reward

it is a constant struggle
to befriend the oceanic
what with its moaning fossils
inconstant moon & rain

some forms of purification kill & sometimes
only brushes with death
can paint a true vista
of the intentional life
not all love is an anchor
the heart has a right
to disembark

III.

colonial grandfathers who collectively gave us
the world of clocks & the killing
of time & pelts both human & animal—
I forgive you pray for us

both now & at the hour of our health
amidst the rare moments of triumph & delight

    we shall be delivered
    from the dark embryo of our lack

it is the fate of our hybrid kin forever
my sisters whom I have never met

who have never seen
beyond their physiognomy—
pray for our forgotten

psychologies, our bodies forced into
soulless places, pray that we will be saved
from you & your ringing bells
for not all who wander...

IV.

as below so above

despite all this underwater wilderness
& thrownness
listen closely & you can always

hear the quiet
crepuscular sound
of thanks

LETTER TO THE BELOVED

Without
your love I am
a heart
that sails

without
purpose I am
as useful as
a ghost who wails

with longing
for the anxious
weight of the
living

LET US COMPARE COSMOLOGIES

after Cohen

You make a girl feel that it's okay
To be in but not of the milky way.

& yes, I have wandered, lonely on purpose
To all your old haunts, hoping you'd surface!

Though it's hard to compare the geometry
Of my people's constant suffering,

I've loved your pristine metaphors
The way they shone like dark citrine.

Yet I wonder: do you ever grieve the way grief
Let you see through what you see?

I dreamt you were dimming
All the lights in paradise.

Wherever you are—pray for us,
Just a line will suffice.

Bless us like you blessed
The world's quintessence

With your song.

TO JOSEPHINE, MY DEAREST SEA NYMPH

I see in your face a moon
          a shy light

dancing over the ages
          a blossom, stark

beauty on the bosom of the world
          a music

of most sanctifying laughter
          & I see also in the dark

pools of your eyes
          a remembrance

of the somatic rooms
          of our youth where

we flirted with endings
          & began

our journey in this mad
          & ravishing world

from dust to stardust
          my floweret, shall

you be my most
          precious friend

MISSISSIPPI GOTHIC

could it be
that I am back in the Mississippi
trying to exorcise

the small & reverent trickster
that brings me to my knees—?
is it necessary I return

to my swarthiest of roots
& darkest of rapids
to feel what's real—?

it will take some time
to unlearn the language of rivers
when you this full of witness

& even then there is
the unmarked grave of the sky
that gets you every time

THE MOOR'S LAMENT

O hunger
buried
in hunger

O shame
buried
in thirst

O curse
of Ham, of being
the first

DÉJÀ VOODOO

like reading the bible every time your heart
breaks & expecting God to accept. Or the incredulous
operatic tear you worry will smudge your Russian
red lipstick or pull your insanity apart,
matryoshka style. Again & again you unfold

until each part of you struggles to breathe in the world
& yet you pretend there is something sensual
about deathdrive & still you flirt
with martyrdom aka the worst form of pride.
You want & you want & forget the shepherd

you prayed to all those years & you have
perfected the art of fooling others & yet only you
know what it all really means: that you're sick,
that your cells are dying over & in the name
of all that is unholy & suddenly your religion

becomes a source of pain. Still you rise,
undeserving, until the pains grow small enough
to get out of bed with & eventually you are even okay
with pain & prefer it over no pain & this

may be the only wisdom that does not come
with age—followed by the moment you extract
all that has destroyed you until what remains
is what you desire & what you desire is what you give
& what you give is the will to live & you want to live.

BLACK HUMOUR(S)

if at times
we look weary

it is because
of the weight

of our quantum
purpose

the hysterical
effluvia

of all that
unused life

our very phlegm
is requiem

WAXING GOLD

let them attach
to our dazzling
symbols

let them
keep our
manuscripts

it's hard to
contain
a cadence that

came before
time
had a name

it's hard
to confine
the divine

GRAVITY & GRACE

a survival love poem

there is gravity
& then there is grace—

let us abolish the distance
between knowing & knowing

with everything we are; our weakness
is we forget to feed on the light—

grace is ascension,
as well as lowering one's self

to see things as they are: men will be alone
in their revolt

in this way their all-knowing clairvoyance
a kind of false "reason," or ether—

in chemistry, this means flammable
anesthetic; in literature, something akin to the sky

I long to ask men to trip on liberty
& then tell me

what are stars & why not mars
& why on earth & why us

having forgotten rational
freedom, the rest of us rejoice

in captivity, are captivated
by the sky's black spaces instead

we stand as beloveds would or should,
dancing around dark matter—

I imagined us otherwise,
& not as others to each other

but perhaps that is how the bell tolls:
dreams are revealed

upon our quivering eyelids
as we sleep to rouse the infinite

space between what we desire—
on the one hand, stars—

& an everlasting idealism, clenching
to the vision of lighter days

many of us have heard
how what matters is

how you relinquish
imaginary advantages

until your only vantage
point is the sun

to save us, I must imagine
you are other

than what you imagine yourself
to be—let us call this forgiveness

or renewal, a kind of strange Spring;
let us find new talismans

or tales, new
songs of ourselves to sing.

TIME IS A WHITE LIE, TRAVEL A VEIL

O SAY CAN YOU SEA

written upon hearing President Barack Obama establish the first marine national monument in the Atlantic Ocean off Cape Cod, September 2016

You designated our first national monument
underneath the sea today, a subaqueous kingdom

the size of Connecticut. There are mermaids
across county lines who will miss you.

Before your reign above water ends I
pray the nation stays afloat. Though you

& I both know all nations float. That there is so much
more than meets the eye & that life is greater than

the sum of its territories or even memories.
Mr. President maybe I will meet you in Hawaii

when you are no longer president but instead
a full-blown mermaid, sailing through your native land.

There we'll be free to talk politics of spirit over poi
& fuschia tea. Or more realistically we will cry

tears melding with the Atlantic, staring out as far as possible
for as long as our squinting eyes can take it.

GHOSTS OF POMPEII

O molten ash,
sulfuric gas—where was Jesu
          at your Vesuvius—

I ask centuries later because I am feeling
that feeling I can only describe as
a difficulty rising above.

          Part of me wants the darkness, all of it
the heat & chalices, courage supreme.
& maybe a cornucopia of fruits
just before the storm.
          I want all forms of extravagance

to be the vagrant sermon on your mount
          a treatise to the bruises
on my knees for the nights I spent the hours
wasting time on attitudes
so mortal & so now.
          Love candles while you can,

dream in Roman tongue & terra
cotta & do not fear the smell of burning bones.
Welcome to my love, equal
          parts ash & delirium, born
from an age where all that glittered
was not gold. It was also
my strega grandmothers
          with their lachrymose
laughter & what have you.

It is a grape stain, broken vessel
in the eye, broken ship
upon waters high
& it is also fires low,
unrepentant.

THE CAPTURED SIREN

writes a letter with fingers in the sand,
nets herself, bears a shadow
on a sunlit day, ponders the end

of her serial geography—her vertiginous
hair aflame on a dark sun, remains maroon
with vertigo, having learned the human

meaning & tinge of morning's cringe,
the impossibility of arrival
in the same old masculine dawn

her fate sealed into a bottled
ship—the only type that voyages
without meaning—she contemplates

with the fishes the meaning of tide,
upturning, pilgrimage, considers
plunging faster than you can say *Look!*

deciphers a way to rise above
the nuisance of a body,
for they may try to contain her

but soon she will be an aria of sea-
foam, soon she will be a mutiny
of light

THE RECKONING

the grotesque
process of becoming yourself
wave by wave:
            the unfolding

first of pain & the promise
of exultation
followed by the sad determinism
            of your old skins & haunts

slowly the acceptance
of the mysterious & holy sounds
that seem to reach you
            from the excessive heavens

asking you bear witness
to who you will become
learn to swim
            eyes open into yourself

at the heart of it
you may always feel
heavy as a cavernous ship
            combined with the dark marina

of your mind
but we are each here
scathed & miraculous
            you'll figure it out

it may go something like this

if the art in you lives
you'll live

LIBERTY SHELL / I HEAR THE OCEAN

for Philadelphia on the centenary of the 1918 race riot

I.

I left you to find independence
from the repetition of primeval values & sacrosanct airs
of bearded men all trying for Whitman,
white men galore.
            I left to find Baraka's ghost
though such proved difficult—after dying he left America in a huff
& left me waiting for trains, boxes full of more men
vying for Whitman.
            I left you to keep the futurity
of my scholarship close but found myself
wishing I could attend Neruda's
university of the waves instead—
            & all the black white noise & how I quivered
with a liberty that left me at a loss
& continuously losing it in public bathrooms
while my ancestors shifted around in their graves.
            I feared you would forever be
an old boys' club—brotherly, but without the shimmering
gold of the Greeks, without love also for women.
            I never quite realized I was
black until I met you. I often feel the curse
of having to stand outside love.
            I still love however your magic
gardens & make-believe desire to make beautiful
that which has been discarded
& your arboretums, the emerald Oz of your
parks & cathedrals scented by papal robes & sweaty

boxing gloves & admiration—
      maybe we can try again when
I have learned to love myself
& stop caring to be adored.
      I admit: I was wrong trying to set up shop
in the spiritually impoverished
corner of my life. Let us call it a reunion & leave the rest
to the love after which you were named
that you can hear in the fragile
distance, like the ocean
in a shell.

II.

I cannot help
but think of the terrible possibility
that not all of us
seek ascension, or were permitted to

or worse, wanted an audience
to cheer us on
as we'd approach paradise—

I am thinking of strange fruit
I am thinking of Waco, Texas
I am saying it how it is & in

a language of blood; keeping
in mind that not all of us who survived
wanted ascesis; wanted instead

all that was
slippery & reptilian
& strange—

I remember many a communion
stuck to the roof of my mouth, my crosses
only half-bore, & the pain
impossible

feats of awake, shower, & proceed
(& somehow breathe)
in all this proverbial black sea

while in prayer my head bends
sinister with the bends & my hands
fumble with the beads.

Lord is it true
that freedom comes to those who are free
& that I may not be?

III.

Or maybe, just maybe
Jesus was secretly mulatto,
born to a small black church at the beginning

of all beginnings, long before
the Song of Songs & white-
washing that would lead

to the ethnic cleansing & passing,
the strange & slippery
color lines of our ancestors

that crossed
& bled
into one another,

unforgiving.

TEETOTALING STUDY

1.

The vast sky reachable, total,
almost intimate. A red-blue bag

of bread that you will actually eat,
maybe feel kind enough to give

to the birds, any birds. The amber light
of a home where all acts of kneeling

& keeling over are for prayer only.
It is the warmest place you want

to be today, Lady Day herself floats by,
winking, a diamond tear in her third eye

& you wink back, without sunglasses,
craving dawn. Flags down, the body

no longer under siege by a totalitarian
state made of castles of trash-green glass.

Your nation no longer floats on firewater—
you are sovereign, preoccupied with temperance & song

& other more motherly things. You have lost your tail
between the legs, grown wings instead, float

atop jazz notes actually noted this time & notebooks
full again to the tune of kettles whistling flirtatious,

siren-like, calling you in for your daily tidal
wave of tea. The kitchen filial, now, the belly

full, not swollen. Your mind a spark, a rose,
sunlit & electric, the shade of free: think juicy pink dress

against a backdrop of turquoise green—age ain't a thing—
the clocks are smiling & you've got that swing—

your hellos deliberate now, amens even
more so, as you think

I shall not want
            the old shell song of myself

& you drown willingly into the majestic
waters of thanks.

2.

Since leaving you

I found again

the hot blue sky

of my future

&

the chords of my
heart

began to sing
with the *not yet*

&

with a certain mimicry

of the fauna
of the sea

I summoned to
release

the past

in a series of heaves

&

in all shades of hepatic
alarm

Soon you will go on

to wreck
some other

life

with an appeal

to the romantic

but there is

nothing beautiful
about

becoming
a shell

about having
nothing left

with which
to plumb the light

except the

last extant
part

of you that decides

it's either ride
the brutal

tides or
die

Since removing you

from my life

I found
alive

UNDERWATER IMPALE: OR, A CONJURING

to impart myself is to impale
            myself exorcize what is dark

& enter the void of this skin & my pain
            is my pain is my blood beating

in the ear of the earth my
            pain is the earth & my love

is a mix of tears, sweat
            & sea & I pray for the things

I can't unsee & I pray
            for the things I can't unsee

to impart myself is to impale
            myself & my love

is a mix of tears sweat & sea
            exorcize what is dark &

enter the void of this skin in the ear
            of the earth my pain

is the earth & my pain is my pain
            is my blood beating & my

pain is my pain is my blood
            beating & I pray for the things

I can't unsee in the ear
            of the earth, my pain is the earth

to impart myself is to impale
myself exorcize what is dark

& enter the void of this skin
& my love is a mix of tears

sweat & sea & my love is
a mix of tears sweat

& sea & my pain
is my pain is my blood

beating exorcize what is dark
& enter the void of this skin

& I pray for the things
I can't unsee to impart

myself is to impale myself
in the ear of the earth

my pain is the earth
in the ear of the earth

my pain is the earth & my love is a
mix of tears sweat & sea to impart

myself is to impale myself & my pain is
my pain is my blood beating & I

pray for the things I can't unsee
exorcize what is dark & enter

the void of this skin
        exorcize what is dark

& enter the void of this
        skin in the ear

of the earth my pain
        is the earth

& I pray for the things
        I can't

unsee & my love
        is a mix of tears sweat & sea

& my pain is my pain
        is my blood beating to impart myself

is to impale myself & my love
        is a mix of tears

sweat & sea & my pain
        is my pain is my

blood
        beating

IN THE WAKE

to say one swims is to say
one stays in life

to live is to stay
in the wake

to stay in the hold
of the ship, holding on

seeking resolution always
for the problemata of your face

the ongoing abjection
which is to say your

stain as in the wake
as in the track left on the surface

of water by a ship
you leave a trace of darkness

you live in the wake
as in disturbance caused by a body swimming

a region of disturbed flow,
your mind a trillion corals

not long ago you
modeled yourself after rivers

ancient rivers
until you decided this life

was too short to be your wake
as in death ritual

as in you chose to live
as in forgive those who hurt you

as in forgive yourself for living
but never apologize for it

as in you will never forget

as in it does get better

as in stay

THE UNMOORING: A PRELUDE

"And there we stand / all the damned of the earth"
— J. Roumain

A body isn't free

until it

has to be

★

We have left the ports

of memory & grief

& abandoned the wreckage

of our disbelief

for the hour has come

for a mending & a

breaking—at turns

committed at turns forsaking

we were resigned

to one life we thought

but now we are taking our

rightful place in the spectra

while those who try & wrest

us may find themselves

distraught—don't they know

that sacrifice

is just another word

for release

that the body's just

a means didn't they

know this gift called life

is an evaluation

★

At first
it will be a menacing

sight to see

the troubled
remembering
their talents

the wronged
deciding
to heal

Where we were
once unwell

there shall be
an unfinished tale

Where there was
          once a wound

a message:

                    our methods

          will be equal

                    parts fulfillment &

          betrayal & we will leave

                              an unruly trail

★

& we won't fail—
We will fight
          to forge a being

out of the void
We will peel back
    the viscera

of our former
selves to reveal
    the not-so-tragic curvature

of our future life—

    Behold how salient
our sails
    & sharp the prisms
of our once-disorganized
            light

    Behold—!
the shifting
    peninsula of our patience
the perilous
dusky reach

    Of our largesse—!

Only a fool
would dare try repress

    the grand design
of our self-
            deliverance

Soon they will
be in awe
of how we
gleam like a continuum
of sun

how we tread
unhurried & even
eloquent
in the aftermath

how we love
without dread
& are
in fact dancing, laughing

the way God laughs
at the gaunt prayer

of the
wicked

ACKNOWLEDGEMENTS

To my family, first & foremost, without whom this voyage would not have been possible—you are loved—& to Pavel, the captain of my heart.

To my friends & colleagues & comrades near & far—your support is a lighthouse.

To Charles Bernstein, Liz Howard, & George Elliott Clarke—enchanté.

To the Ontario Arts Council, for their generous support during the writing of this book.

Finally, to Denis on behalf of Mansfield Press—infinite thanks for believing in me through the years, & for your patience & generosity.

Poems from this collection previously appeared in *ROOM*, the *White Wall Review*, *The Wanderer*, *Minola Review*, *Juniper*, and *Cosmonauts Avenue*.

Adebe DeRango-Adem was called a young Canadian author to watch in 2016 by Canada's parliamentary poet laureate, George Elliott Clarke. A former student of Anne Waldman and Amiri Baraka through the Jack Kerouac School of Disembodied Poetics at Naropa University, Adebe is the author of two full-length poetry collections: *Ex Nihilo* and *Terra Incognita*. *Ex Nihilo* was nominated for the prestigious Dylan Thomas Prize, while her most recent book, *Terra Incognita*, published in 2015, was a finalist for the Pat Lowther award. Poems from the collection were also long-listed for the inaugural Cosmonauts Avenue Poetry Prize, as judged by award-winning American poet Claudia Rankine. She is currently an English doctoral student at the University of Pennsylvania.

Selected Titles From Mansfield Press

Poetry

Leanne Averbach, *Fever*
Tara Azzopardi, *Last Stop, Lonesome Town*
Nelson Ball, *In This Thin Rain*
Nelson Ball, *Some Mornings*
Nelson Ball, *Chewing Water*
Nelson Ball, *Walking*
Gary Barwin, *Moon Baboon Canoe*
Samantha Bernstein, *Spit on the Devil*
George Bowering, *Teeth: Poems 2006–2011*
Stephen Brockwell, *All of Us Reticent, Here, Together*
Stephen Brockwell, *Complete Surprising Fragments of Improbable Books*
Alice Burdick, *Book of Short Sentences*
Alice Burdick, *Flutter*
Alice Burdick, *Holler*
Sarah Burgoyne, *Saint Twin*
Jason Camlot, *What The World Said*
Pino Coluccio, *First Comes Love*
Marie-Ève Comtois, *My Planet of Kites*
Dani Couture, *YAW*
Gary Michael Dault, *The Milk of Birds*
Frank Davey, *Poems Suitable to Current Material Conditions*
Pier Giorgio Di Cicco, *Dead Men of the Fifties*
Pier Giorgio Di Cicco, *My Life Without Me*
Pier Giorgio Di Cicco, *The Visible World*
Pier Giorgio Di Cicco, *Wishipedia*
Christopher Doda, *Aesthetics Lesson*
Christopher Doda, *Glutton for Punishment*
Glen Downie, *Monkey Soap*
Rishma Dunlop, *Lover Through Departure: New and Selected Poems*
Rishma Dunlop & Priscila Uppal, eds., *Red Silk: An Anthology of South Asian Women Poets*
Puneet Dutt, *The Better Monsters*
Laura Farina, *Some Talk of Being Human*
Jaime Forsythe, *Sympathy Loophole*
Eva HD, *Rotten Perfect Mouth*
Eva HD, *Shiner*
Jason Heroux, *Hard Work Cheering Up Sad Machines*
Jason Heroux, *Natural Capital*
John B. Lee, *In the Terrible Weather of Guns*
Jeanette Lynes, *The Aging Cheerleader's Alphabet*
David W. McFadden, *Abnormal Brain Sonnets*
David W. McFadden, *Be Calm, Honey*
David W. McFadden, *Shouting Your Name Down the Well: Tankas and Haiku*
David W. McFadden, *What's the Score?*
Kathryn Mockler, *The Purpose Pitch*
Nathaniel, G. Moore, *Goodbye Horses*
Leigh Nash, *Goodbye, Ukulele*
Lillian Necakov, *The Bone Broker*
Lillian Necakov, *Hooligans*
Peter Norman, *At the Gates of the Theme Park*
Peter Norman, *Water Damage*
Natasha Nuhanovic, *Stray Dog Embassy*
Catherine Owen & Joe Rosenblatt, *Dog*
Corrado Paina, *Cinematic Taxi*
Corrado Paina, *The Dowry of Education*
Nick Papaxanthos, *Love Me Tender*
Branka Petrovic, *Mechanics of a Gaze*
Shannon Quinn, *Nightlight for Children of Insomniacs*
Stuart Ross et al., *Our Days in Vaudeville*
Jim Smith, *Back Off, Assassin! New and Selected Poems*
Jim Smith, *Happy Birthday, Nicanor Parra*
Robert Earl Stewart, *Campfire Radio Rhapsody*
Robert Earl Stewart, *Something Burned along the Southern Border*
Meaghan Strimas, *Yes Or Nope*
Carey Toane, *The Crystal Palace*
Aaron Tucker, *Punchlines*
Priscila Uppal, *Sabotage*
Priscila Uppal, *Summer Sport: Poems*
Priscila Uppal, *Winter Sport: Poems*
Steve Venright, *Floors of Enduring Beauty*
Brian Wickers, *Stations of the Lost*
Tara-Michelle Ziniuk, *Whatever, Iceberg*

Fiction

Marianne Apostolides, *The Lucky Child*
Sarah Dearing, *The Art of Sufficient Conclusions*
Salvatore Difalco, *Mean Season*
Paula Eisenstein, *Flip Turn*
Sara Heinonen, *Dear Leaves, I Miss You All*
Jason Heroux. *Amusement Park of Constant Sorrow*
Kasia Jaronczyk, *Lemons*
Christine Miscione, *Carafola*
Marko Sijan, *Mongrel*
Tom Walmsley, *Dog Eat Rat*
Corinne Wasilewski, *Live from the Underground*

Non-Fiction

George Bowering, *How I Wrote Certain of My Books*
Mark Cirilo, *Pizza Cultura*
Pier Giorgio Di Cicco, *Municipal Mind: Manifestos for the Creative City*
Amy Lavender Harris, *Imagining Toronto*
David W. McFadden, *Mother Died Last Summer*
Deborah Verginella, ed., *Buon Appetito Toronto!*

For a complete list of Mansfield Press titles, please visit mansfieldpress.net